QUANTUM READING

The Power to Read Your Best

by

Bobbi DePorter

with Mike Hernacki

Learning Forum Publications
Oceanside, California USA

LEARNING FORUM PUBLICATIONS
1725 South Coast Highway
Oceanside, CA 92054-5319 USA
(760) 722-0072
(760) 722-3507 fax
email: info@learningforum.com
www.learningforum.com

Cover design by Kelley Thomas
Illustrations by Ellen Duris

ISBN: 0-945525-23-0

*Dedicated to all the very special Learning Forum staff
who over the years have contributed so much.*

The Power to
Read Your Best

? *What are three key ways to increase speed and comprehension?*

? *Why is an alpha brain-wave state beneficial for reading?*

? *How can you increase your peripheral vision?*

? *What one thing can you do that will double your reading speed?*

Contents

1

Why?
Motivation for Reading

Time. There just never seems to be enough of it. The fast pace of life leaves more and more of us juggling jobs, school, family, friends, physical fitness, and community service. With so many commitments to fulfill, it's no wonder we sometimes drop the ball.

One of the balls we drop more than the others is the stack of reading material that seems to be breeding and reproducing itself in the corner. "If I only had the time to read," you say to yourself, "I could keep abreast of current trends and innovations, and all the required reading I have to do. But how can I create time? There are only so many hours . . . ."

True, you can't create time; there are only so many hours in a day. If all you have is 20 minutes a day for informational reading, but you really need two hours, you'll just keep falling farther and farther behind. On the other hand, if you could increase your speed and comprehension so that you got two hours' worth of reading done in 20 minutes, not only would you breeze through that stack of papers, you'd also free up more time for other aspects of life you may be neglecting—family, friends, or fitness.

Perhaps there's something you've been yearning to do, but you've kept putting it off because there doesn't seem to be time. Maybe it's taking a class or learning something new. You've told yourself that with full-time school or work you just can't do it. But what if you could breeze through your school or work assignments in a few minutes? What possibilities would that open up for you?

If you learn to use Whole Brain Quantum Reading Skills explained in this chapter, you'll not only save lots of time, you'll also get your life in better balance. Plus, the large amounts of information you'll be able to absorb in a short time will open up new opportunities. The faster you read,

Mastery of Whole Brain Quantum Reading skills has many benefits.

What's In It For Me:

Read more in less time

::

Increase your comprehension
and recall

::

Gain opportunities

::

Get your life in balance

the easier it is to keep all those balls in the air without dropping any.

Steve Snyder, international trainer and consultant, reads four books per night in addition to all his "To Read" materials from work. He reads at a rate of about 5,000 words per minute—10,000 when he's in a hurry. His mother taught him to read when he was two, and by the time he entered first grade, he was reading at a high school level. He began speed-reading when he was 12, using techniques he had developed himself. Soon he was teaching his friends how to cut their study time in half with speed-reading.

We all have the capacity to read as quickly as Steve. In fact, our brains want to read quickly, but we usually slow things down, thinking that if we read slowly, we'll understand the material better. In reality, this can have the opposite effect. Reading slowly can be boring, and when we slow down our minds wander and we miss information.

Have you ever read something you urgently needed to know when time was short, like information for a report or license exam? When you studied as your deadline loomed, you probably shut out all distractions and focused completely on your material. You read as if your life depended on it. And with that high level of focus you retained more information than usual. You were focused because you were interested in succeeding.

We all read better and retain more when our interest is high. Whole Brain Quantum Reading is based on the concept of recapturing a highly focused state each time we read. Fast reading requires this high level of focused concentration, because it's when our minds are engaged and active that comprehension increases.

Whole Brain Quantum Reading uses both sides of the brain more effectively. Brain researchers agree that nearly

Our brains want to read quickly.

*Fast reading requires a high level
of focused concentration.
When our minds are engaged and active,
comprehension increases.*

an unlimited number of neural connections are possible. By employing both the left and right hemispheres, we can use more of that potential, increasing speed and comprehension to higher levels than we ever thought possible.

When we read, we primarily use the left hemisphere. This is the logical, analytical hemisphere which we use for language tasks like writing and reading. The right hemisphere is holistic, rhythmic, colorful, imaginative, and creative. To effectively engage the right hemisphere while reading, we need to use a few Quantum Reading strategies. For example, try visualizing the material, listening to baroque music while you read, or making the material more meaningful by relating it to something in your own life. Getting into a relaxed, focused state also helps you use both sides of your brain. You'll learn more about this later in this book.

But before we delve into the reading process, let's measure your current reading rate. When you've completed this book, rate yourself again and compare the two scores to see how much your reading has improved. To do this exercise, you'll need a stopwatch or an electronic wristwatch with a chronometer. Read the book excerpt that starts on page 45 for one minute exactly, then mark the last line you read. Start now.

Now you're ready to master the two building blocks of Quantum Reading: state and skills. "State" is your state of mind, your focus, and your physiology. The skills you need are eye and hand techniques.

Speed and comprehension increase by using techniques that employ both left and right hemispheres.

Increase right hemisphere activities by:

Visualizing the material

::

Listening to baroque music

::

Relating it to something personal

::

Getting into a relaxed, focused state

2

Getting Into An
Effective Reading State

The ABC's of State

Attitude

Attitude includes both your feelings about something and the conscious adjustment of your physical posture to reflect those feelings. Before you can read at top speeds, you must think and act like a Quantum Reader.

If you dislike reading or find it a chore, you must first dump all the old, negative ideas you may be carrying around with you. Imagine yourself tossing away thoughts like, "I'm a slow reader; I hate reading; I always did poorly at reading in school; I hate those boring reports I have to read; I get embarrassed when I have to read to others." Open the window, pretend you're physically picking up these thoughts one by one, then "toss" them out and watch them drift away. Be sure all your old ideas about reading have been tossed. Then sit up straight, tall and proud. Adjust your posture to reflect your new attitude. Open your mind to new possibilities and get ready to take on some new beliefs.

Belief

As with most Quantum Learning activities, to read faster and comprehend better you need to engage the limitless power of your mind. You must believe that you can do it; you can change the way you read; you can read four books a night if you choose to. In the words of Henry Ford, "If you believe you can, you can, and if you believe you can't, you can't. Either way, you are right."

Replace the old beliefs you just tossed out with these new, positive, effective thoughts: "I am a powerful reader! I read quickly and understand thoroughly." Close your eyes, relax, and repeat these words out loud. Let them sink into your subconscious mind. Imagine yourself powering

Think and act like a
Quantum Reader.

The ABC's of State:

Attitude –   Sit up and open your mind to new possibilities.

Belief –   Replace old beliefs with new, positive thoughts, such as "I am a powerful reader".

Concentration –   Focus your mind by accessing the alpha-brain wave state.

Commitment –   Commit to practicing your new skills.

through assignments and reports quickly and effortlessly. See yourself having time to read the newspaper and other publications, and being up to date on the latest break-throughs. How much time can you save through Quantum Reading and how will you spend it? Believe in the power and potential of using your whole brain, and you'll read faster and with greater comprehension than you could ever have imagined.

Concentration and Commitment

Focused concentration is a key ingredient if you want to read at Quantum rates and understand what you read. It's part of the state of being a Quantum Reader. In earlier chapters we mentioned how people learn more quickly and easily when they're in a relaxed, focused state. To focus your mind you need to access the alpha brain wave state. The alpha state is one of four states of brain wave activity measured on an electroencephalograph (EEG). As you may know, electrical activity in the brain fluctuates from high to low. Here's a quick run-down on the four brain wave states and their corresponding activities.

Beta

Awake, alert, and active. In beta, your brain is attending to many different stimuli at once and activity is scattered. You may be thinking of many things at the same time or jumping from one activity to another, such as reading a report, thinking about other things that need to be done, half-listening to someone else's conversation, and jumping up to answer the phone.

Alpha

A state of concentration or daydreaming. You're relaxed and alert; you're absorbing material. You're focused on one activity, such as playing a challenging

Electrical activity in the brain fluctuates from high to low.

Brain Wave States:

Beta	Alert and active, thinking of many things at once
Alpha	Relaxed and alert, absorbing information
Theta	Almost asleep, dreaming to deep hypnosis
Delta	Deep sleep

game of chess. This is the state we want to access for optimum Quantum Reading.

Theta

Brain waves are slowing down. You're almost asleep, in a light sleep, dreaming, or in deep hypnosis.

Delta

The slowest brain wave state. Your metabolic processes have slowed and you're in a deep sleep.

The alpha state is the best state for learning. In order to quickly access a relaxed state every time you read, start by doing the following visualization:

Close your eyes and think of a place and time where you felt relaxed and at peace. It could be a favorite vacation spot or a special room at home. Picture yourself in this place and feel yourself relaxing. Do this for a few minutes to anchor this thought in your mind. You're now entering into an alpha brain wave state.

You should be able to return to this state quickly just by closing your eyes and thinking of the special place you pictured in the visualization. Try it again now.

Your brain takes cues from your body and the position you're in. To improve concentration, try adopting a focused physiology. If you're slouched in your chair, your brain interprets this as boredom. If you're lying down, your brain thinks it's time to sleep and chemicals are released that make you sleepy. Just as skiers or tennis players take a certain stance to perform their best, you must adopt the stance of an excellent reader.

Now, sit up straight in your chair with both feet on the floor. Take a deep breath. Think of your peaceful place. Close your eyes and roll them up in your head; this puts you in a visual mode. Then open your eyes and look down

The Alpha brain-wave state is the best state for learning.

To quickly access an alpha state:

Sit up

::

Take a deep breath

::

Close your eyes and roll them up

::

Think of your peaceful place

::

Open your eyes and look at your book

at your book. Practice this a few times, so that you can go into alpha quickly. Remember to go through these steps every time you're about to read.

Learning any new skill takes a certain amount of practice and commitment. How much are you willing to commit? To find out, take a sheet of paper, and copy the formula on the page to the right.

Under the word "Commit," write the number, on a scale of one to ten, that represents how much you'll dare to commit to your new reading skills. A "10" means you're willing to apply yourself at your top capacity; you're willing to commit your best efforts, without hesitation or reservation. A "1" means you're not that keen on it, or that you'll put a little effort into it if you have nothing else to do.

Now, under the word "Change," indicate the amount you'll dare to be open to changing your old ways of reading, again on a scale of one to ten. How much will you dare to believe that you'll learn new ways to read, read faster, and with greater comprehension? How much will you dare to believe in yourself, in your untapped potential? Multiply these numbers together and you'll get your ABC's Quotient of Reading Success.

You are responsible for your reading success. How much are you willing to commit?

Your ABC's Quotient of Reading Success

Commit   _____
                (write a number from 1 to 10)

Change x _____
                (write a number from 1 to 10)

Quotient _____%
                (this is the level of your commitment)

3

Eye & Hand Skills

N ow you have a positive attitude and new beliefs about your ability to read. You've committed your-self to trying something new and know how to access a state of focused concentration. It's time to learn the eye and hand skills—the next step to becoming a Quantum Reader.

Eye Skills

Following are several exercises to help you learn how to move your eyes in new ways across the page. Most of us read one word at a time. Our minds, however, can compre-hend much more. The words have greater meaning for us when we see them together in groups because they are then in context. In order to see more than one word at once, we need to use our peripheral vision.

To test your peripheral vision, put your arms straight out in front of you with your hands in a fist, thumbs up. Slowly move your hands out to each side, keeping your eyes straight ahead. Stop your arms just before your thumbs get out of view. Most people can see up to 45 degrees in each direction from straight ahead, using only their peripheral vision. If this is true for you, that means your range of vision without moving your eyes is 90 degrees.

Here's another exercise: Look at the right-hand page. Focus your eyes on the letter "A" in the center of the alphabet, and find which letter you can see out to without moving your eyes. Can you see out to "D", "G" or all the way to "J"? As you practice Quantum Reading, your periph-eral vision will improve. Return to this exercise after you've practiced a bit, and measure how much farther you can see.

Soft Focus

Focusing your eyes a different way can help you see

We use our peripheral vision to see more at one time.

```
J J J J J J J J J J J J J J J J J J
J I I I I I I I I I I I I I I I I I J
J I H H H H H H H H H H H H H H I J
J I H G G G G G G G G G G G G G H I J
J I H G F F F F F F F F F F F G H I J
J I H G F E E E E E E E E E F G H I J
J I H G F E D D D D D D D E F G H I J
J I H G F E D C C C C C D E F G H I J
J I H G F E D C B B B C D E F G H I J
J I H G F E D C B A B C D E F G H I J
J I H G F E D C B B B C D E F G H I J
J I H G F E D C C C C C D E F G H I J
J I H G F E D D D D D D D E F G H I J
J I H G F E E E E E E E E E F G H I J
J I H G F F F F F F F F F F F G H I J
J I H G G G G G G G G G G G G G H I J
J I H H H H H H H H H H H H H H I J
J I I I I I I I I I I I I I I I I I J
J J J J J J J J J J J J J J J J J J
```

more words at once. One way is called "soft focus." Practice soft focus by putting your attention on the white spaces between the lines of text. As you read line by line, follow the white space rather than the letters themselves. Let your peripheral vision see the line above the white space. This exercise expands your peripheral vision so you take in more text at once. It's also easier on the eyes and results in less eye fatigue.

Tri-Focus

This is a method of seeing groups of words instead of single words. Imagine that each line of type is divided into thirds, with the words clumped into three groups. As you read, let your eyes jump from group to group instead of from word to word, reading several words in a group at once. To practice, look at the tri-focus exercise on the right page. Time yourself to see how much faster you read using this method. You can also practice this method any time you like with an imaginary book. Close your eyes and move them left, center, right, repeatedly. Snap your fingers to the rhythm. Do this any time you have a few minutes—when standing in line at the supermarket, sitting in the doctor's waiting room, or other similar situations.

Both soft focus and tri-focus exercises help you learn to read groups of words and develop your peripheral vision. It's going to take some practice to break the old habit of reading one word at a time, though; after all, you've probably been doing it since you learned to read. So stick with the new methods and they'll soon pay off.

The Military Origins of Speed-Reading

The idea of using a quick focus was actually developed by the United States Air Force when tacticians noticed that some pilots were unable to distinguish different kinds of

Tri-Focus:
Practice reading several words together in a group.

The world, as a global
and is accelerating.
of students from diverse
from one another.
international SuperCamps
Forum we envisioned
parts of the world. At
going to happen; it felt
comes as a surprise
national programs
ging so fast, at times
remember distinctly the
phone call was a big
side of the world
into my office and
England who wants the
camp enrollment forms
minutes. We have a
dents attending our U.S.
world have become
porters. Our global
was written years ago,
priate than ever. An
tating a shift in
tive, responsible people
For change to happen
gether. Our international
In England, students
nationalities come
In Moscow, 1990, our
overwhelmed by the

community, has
I have experienced
cultures coming
This is the type of
provide. When we
SuperCamp pro-
that time we didn't
like a lofty goal.
that we arrived at
continue to expand.
it's challenging to
days when making
event, and sending
required weeks to
receive a phone call
address of someone
are being emailed to
growing number of
programs. People
good friends and
community is here
our company vision
international model
learning, resulting
participating in a
in the world, we
programs serve to
from a variety of
together with new
first international
generosity of the

gained momentum
firsthand the value
together to learn
opportunity our
started Learning
grams in many
know how this was
Today, it almost
our goal and inter-
The world is chan-
stay in step. I
a long distance
a letter to the other
arrive. Today I step
from a parent in
in New York, while
France, arriving in
international stu-
from around the
SuperCamp sup-
today. Although it
seems more appro-
of excellence, facili-
in educated, crea-
global community.
need to work to-
further this change.
backgrounds and
understanding.
program, we were
host families.

planes from a distance. In the life-and-death situation of combat, this inability to tell one plane from another was obviously an enormous disadvantage, so Air Force psychologists and educators set about to remedy the situation. They developed a machine called a tachistoscope, which is simply a device that flashes images for varying periods of time on a large screen. They started by flashing fairly large pictures of friendly and enemy aircraft at very slow exposures, then gradually shortened the exposure while decreasing the size of the image. To their surprise, they found that, with training, the average person was able to distinguish almost speck-like representations of different planes when the images had been flashed on the screen for only one five-hundredth of a second.

Reasoning that the perceptual ability of the eyes had been vastly underrated, they decided to transfer this information to reading. Using exactly the same device and process, they first flashed one large word for as long as five seconds on a screen, then gradually reduced the size of the word while shortening the length of the flash. This they were able to do until they were flashing four words simultaneously on a screen for one five-hundredth of a second, and readers were still able to recognize the words.

Others adopted this approach, and most speed-reading courses and kits were based on tachistoscopic training. This approach usually provided the student with a graph, graded in units of ten from 100 to 400 words per minute. Most students, with regular training, were able to climb from an average of 200 words per minute to an average of 400. Unfortunately, the graduates of such training schemes reported a general dissatisfaction after several weeks of "postgraduate" reading. An enormous number of them

Your reading speed has a lot to do with your motivation level.

Increasing

or

maintaining

an efficient

reading

speed

is an

ongoing

process.

noticed that shortly after they completed the course, their reading speed sank to the previous level.

Only recently have experts recognized that the normal range of reading ability is roughly 200-400 words per minute, and that most people operate at the lowest level of this range. The increased reading ability observed in the tachistoscopic courses had little to do with the training itself, but was more a function of motivation. The readers were determined to read faster over the weeks of the course and so were able to reach the top of their normal range. But once the course ended, their motivation dropped.

Another explanation for the failure of the still-screen approach is that in order to see something clearly, the eye must be still in relation to the object it is seeing.

Because the words on a page are still, the eye must be still when it is looking at them. But because there are many words to read, the eye must also move. This apparently paradoxical situation, in which the eye is required both to be still and to move, is resolved by putting the two in sequence: The eye must be still to take in a single word or group of words, then must move to the next group of words, and so on. The eye must therefore be trained to move efficiently rather than just seeing flashes.

Hand Skills

When you first learned to read, you ran your finger along the words to keep your place. Later you were told that this isn't the way "big people" read, and that it slows you down. Well, believe it or not, you're going to go back to using your finger again. And don't worry; studies have shown that this method of reading actually increases your speed. Using your finger or a pencil as a visual guide keeps you moving ahead and stops you from backtracking. Sometimes you

Using a visual guide such as your finger keeps your eyes moving ahead.

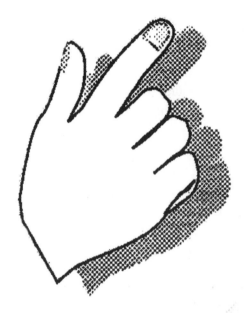

It can double your speed!

may stop and re-read words because you think you didn't get something, but if you're focused, you'll get it. You need to keep moving forward to increase your speed. As your eyes are "pushed" along by your finger, they move across the page faster and more efficiently. This is one of the most effective ways to speed up your reading. Even if you ignore other Quantum Reading skills, you can still double your speed, or more, with a visual guide.

If you want to test whether a guide really makes a difference, try this experiment. Sit face-to-face with a friend, and ask that person to look about six inches above your head and move his eyes around your face, making a circle. (He should move his eyes only, not his head.) Watch his eyes as they move. You'll probably notice that they move in short spurts and jerks.

Now try the exercise again, but this time tell your friend to use his finger as a visual guide. He should hold his finger about three inches from your head and move it in a circle around your face, following his finger with his eyes. His eyes will move smoothly this time because they have something to follow to keep them moving along.

Reading Line-by-Line

Look at the diagram on the next page. It shows the pattern of movement your visual guide should follow when you read line-by-line. Using this pattern, move your finger along the lines of text as you read this book. Your eyes should be just ahead of your finger. As you come to the end of a line, quickly move to the line below. Push yourself to move a little faster than is comfortable for you. Use your peripheral vision to take in a third of a line at once. With practice, you'll pick up speed and improve comprehension.

Line-by-Line Reading

Push yourself to move a little faster
than is comfortable for you.

The Ski or "U" Method

Sometimes, you may not want to read every line; you just want to read very fast and skim the material. To do this, use the ski or "U" method. Using the finger on your right hand as a guide, let your finger "ski" back and forth down the page, like a skier slaloming down the slope. Do this on first the left hand page, then the right. Or, make a "U" pattern spanning both pages. (Don't worry about reading the words at this point; just practice the movements.)

Page-Turning

In order to Quantum Read you have to turn pages at quantum speeds. To do this, sit at a table where you can support the book. Then hold onto the top center of the book with your left hand. Reach over with that same hand and turn the page from the top right corner. Use only your left hand to turn pages; when you're Quantum Reading, you'll be using your right hand as your visual guide. Practice page-turning for a few minutes. Time yourself to see how fast you can go. Fast page-turning improves your reading speed.

Now we'll put your page-turning abilities to the test by combining them with your skiing or U-ing skills. Hold the book and turn pages with your left hand, and ski or "U" with your right. Practice U-ing or skiing and turning pages. See how fast you can go. This method is called "superscan," and you'll use it for your fastest reading. You'll also use it to preview material before you begin more in-depth reading.

You now have all the skills you need to be a Quantum Reader, so let's go over the entire Quantum Reading Process.

Practice these
movement patterns:

"Skiing"

"U"
Method

Practice "Skiing or U-ing as you
also practice page-turning.

4

Putting It All Together
THE WHOLE BRAIN
READING PROCESS

G et out a book or other material you need to read and go through the following steps:

Step One: Prepare

Before you begin reading, prepare your reading area. You'll need good lighting, a comfortable chair, a table to support your book, and colored pens and paper for taking notes. You may also want to include a highlighter, if you like highlighting in your books. I find highlighting to be a great time saver; when I review a book, I simply superscan the highlighted areas.

As you get ready to read, ask questions. "Why am I reading this? What do I expect to learn?" If you ask specific questions about the material, answers will pop out at you as you read. As your mind hunts for the answers, your comprehension increases. I attended a lecture given by Paul Scheele, author of *The PhotoReading Whole Mind System,* (Learning Strategies Corporation, Wayzata, Minnesota, 1993). He said, "Reading is predicting. You could be wrong, and it doesn't matter. It gets you thinking about the material. Ask yourself, 'What would I say if I were going to write this book.'"

Also, decide how much you're going to read before you begin. Most of us have experienced stopping in the middle of our reading to see how much farther we have to go. Get this over with before you start. Decide how much you'll read, then mark the spot with a bookmark. This simple step will free you to concentrate on your reading.

Step Two: Get Into State

Now, use your "ABC's of State." Check your attitude, beliefs, and concentration/commitment. Adopt a positive attitude. Believe in the power of your mind; you can read with lightning speed if you want to. Commit yourself to

Preparing your reading area supports your reading success.

giving 100 percent and trying your new skills. Concentrate fully by accessing alpha state. Sit up straight, breathe deeply, think of your peaceful place, roll your eyes up, then look down.

Step Three: Use Eye and Hand Skills

Remind yourself to use your eye and hand skills. Try soft focus and tri-focus. Concentrate on using peripheral vision to see groups of words at once. Hold the top of your book with your left hand, and use your right hand as a guide.

Step Four: Superscan

Warm up with superscan. First, quickly go through your book from cover to cover, scanning the table of contents, chapter headings, pictures, graphs—anything that stands out. Also, scan the front and back cover, inside flaps, and forward or introduction. Now as fast as you can, use the skiing or U-ing method to go through the pages.

As you Superscan, talk to yourself about what you see in the book. Say to yourself: "What is that? What does it mean? Now the author's talking about this—why?" When you re-read the material you'll already be familiar with it, increasing your comprehension. When you finish, take notes on what you remember. Use Mind Mapping® or other note-taking method. A Mind Map starts with a central idea in the middle of your page with branches for subtopics and details. (Read more about Mind Mapping in *QUANTUM NOTES.*)

Step Five: Read

Now go back and read the material you just super-scanned. Remember to stay in alpha state. If you lose focus, stop immediately and get back into state by going through Step Two again. Use your eye and hand skills. See groups of words, and use a visual guide. Again, keep your

The Whole Brain
Quantum Reading Process

Follow these steps:

1   Prepare

2   Get Into State

3   Use Eye and Hand Skills

4   SuperScan

5   Read

6   Review

concentration and push yourself. At first you may want to stick with line-by-line reading, but as your speed builds you can use the ski or "U" method. Also, you may want to take time to add to your Mind Map, and underline or highlight as you read.

Step Six: Review

When you finish reading, complete your Mind Map. You may also want to try telling someone else about what you read, or talk to yourself. This will help you understand and remember the material. Keep your Mind Map folded in the front of your book. You can read it whenever you need a quick review of the main ideas in the book.

See the diagram on the next page for a visual review. This may help you remember the steps. The top half of the eight represents steps 1-4, the skills you need to practice repeatedly to improve your reading. The entire figure eight is the whole process.

Mastering this process is somewhat like learning to skate a figure-8 on the ice. When I was growing up, I dreamed of being an ice skating star. Every Saturday morning I was at the rink bright and early to practice my "figure-8's". Because I had a poor left edge, my trainer had me do one circle over and over again on my left foot. When I got that down pat, I got to skate the complete figure 8.

Now that you've learned the Whole Brain Quantum Reading Process, repeat the first exercise you did when you timed your initial reading speed. This time continue where you left off in *The Einstein Factor* and see how your reading speed has increased. Then celebrate your achievement!

If you have a large stack of books to catch up on, choose four or five and concentrate on those for a month. Practice

Practice steps 1 – 4
several times before
moving to steps 5 & 6.

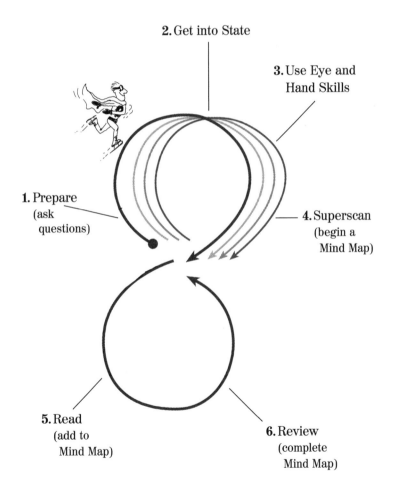

2. Get into State

3. Use Eye and
   Hand Skills

1. Prepare
   (ask
   questions)

4. Superscan
   (begin a
   Mind Map)

5. Read
   (add to
   Mind Map)

6. Review
   (complete
   Mind Map)

improving your speed and concentration by superscanning a book for a few days or a week. Then read and Mind Map it. Rotate in a new book each week. After superscanning, reading, and Mind Mapping, you'll know the material extensively and your Mind Map will serve as a review whenever needed. You'll also get through that stack a lot faster then you ever expected.

If you did the exercises in this book, you've already done a lot to improve your reading. Keep working on increasing your speed and comprehension. I recommend practicing steps 1-4 for five minutes a day. Think of the time you'll save and the possibilities that lie ahead.

Congratulations! Now you're a Quantum Reader.

How to get through
your stack of books:

1. Pick four to five books.

2. Superscan a book for a few
    days or week.

3. Read and Mind Map

4. Rotate in a book each week.

Celebrate Your Learning!

! *What are three key ways that increase speed and comprehension?*

- High interest
- Focused concentration
- Using techniques employing both hemispheres of the brain

! *Why is an alpha brain-wave state beneficial for reading?*

It is a relaxed, yet comfortable state for improved concentration.

! *How can your increase your peripheral vision?*

By practicing "soft focus"—focusing on the white space between the lines and the "tri-focus" exercise—focusing on groups of words.

! *What one thing can you do that will double your reading speed?*

Use a visual guide. It stops you from backtracking. For most effective reading, use the six-step Whole Brain Quantum Reading Process.

Appendix

Reading Test

The Einstein Factor

The Einstein Factor

by Win Wenger, Ph.D., and Richard Poe

Today, those numinous eyes, bushy mustache, and shock of silver hair remain the quintessential image of "genius," the name a synonym for supernormal intelligence. But as a child, Albert Einstein appeared deficient. Dyslexia caused him difficulty in speech and reading.　　5

"Normal childhood development proceeded slowly," recalled his sister. "He had such difficulty with language that they feared that he would never learn to speak... Every sentence he uttered, he repeated to himself, softly, moving his lips. This habit persisted into his　　10 seventh year."

Later, poor language skills provoked his Greek teacher to tell the boy, "You will never amount to anything." Einstein was expelled from high school. He flunked a college entrance exam. After finally completing his bachelor's degree, he failed to attain a recommendation　　15 from his professors and was forced to take a lowly job in the Swiss patent office. Until his mid-20's, he seemed destined for a life of mediocrity. Yet, when he was 26, Einstein published his Special Theory of Relativity. Sixteen years later, he won a Nobel prize.　　20

What did Einstein have that we don't? That's what Dr. Thomas Harvey wanted to know. He was the pathologist on duty at Princeton Hospital when Einstein died in 1955. By sheer chance, fate had fingered Harvey to perform Einstein's autopsy. Without permission from the　　25 family, Harvey took it upon himself to remove and keep Einstein's famous brain. For the next 40 years, Harvey stored the brain in jars of formaldehyde, studying it slice by slice under the microscope and dispersing small samples to other researchers on request.　　30

"Nobody had ever found a difference that earmarked a brain as that of a genius," Harvey later explained to a reporter. Neither he nor his colleagues found any definitive sign that would mark Einstein's brain as extraordinary according to the ideas of brain physiology of that time. But in the early 1980's, Marian Diamond, a neuroanatomist at the University of California at Berkeley, made some discoveries about brains in general and Einstein's in particular that could revolutionize ideas about genius and help entrepreneurs who want to become more innovative.

One of Diamond's experiments was with rats. One group she placed in a super-stimulating environment with swings, ladders, treadmills, and toys. The other group was confined to bare cages. The rats in the big-stimulus environment not only lived to the advanced age of 3 (the equivalent of 90 in a man), but their brains increased in size, sprouting new glial cells, which make connections between neurons (nerve cells). As long ago as 1911, Santiago Ramòn y Cajal, the father of neuroanatomy had found that the number of interconnections between neurons was a far better predictor of brain power than the sheer number of neurons.

So, in rats, Diamond had created the physical footprint of higher intelligence through mental exercise. She then examined sections of Einstein's brain—and found that it, too, was unusually "interconnected." It had a larger-than-normal number of glial cells in the left parietal lobe, which is a kind of neurological switching station that connects the various areas of the brain. It has long been known that unlike neurons, which do not reproduce after we are born, the connective hardware of the brain—glial cells, axons, and dendrites—can increase in number throughout life, depending on how you use your brain. The more we learn, the more of these pathways are 65 created. When we learn a skill such as riding a bicycle, we create connections between brain cells that remain for decades. Mental power is, in a way, connective power.

A "Retarded" Achievement

Was Einstein's mental development affected by some 70 analogy to the swings, ladders, treadmills, and toys of Diamond's super-rats? Did he, in some sense, *learn* his inventive mental powers? Einstein himself seemed to think so. He believed that you could stimulate ingenious thought by allowing the imagination to float freely, form- 75 ing associations at will. For instance, he attributed his Theory of Relativity not to any special gift, but to what he called his "retarded" development.

"A normal adult never stops to think about problems of space and time," he said. "These are things which he has 80 thought of as a child. But my intellectual development was retarded, and I began to wonder about space and time only when I had already grown up."

In his *Autobiographical Notes,* Einstein recalled having the first crucial insight that led to his Special Theory of 85 Relativity at age 16 while he was daydreaming.

As a boy, Einstein had a favorite uncle named Jakob who used to teach him mathematics. "Algebra is a merry science," said Jakob once. "We go hunting for a little ani- mal whose name we don't know, so we call it x. When we 90 bag our game, we pounce on it and give it its right name." Uncle Jakob's words stayed with Einstein for the rest of his life. They encapsulated his attitude toward mathemat- ical and scientific problems, which to Einstein always seemed more like puzzles or games than work. Einstein 95 could focus on his math studies with the concentration most children reserve for play.

"What would it be like," Einstein wondered, "to run beside a light beam at the speed of light?" Normal adults would squelch such a question or forget it. Einstein was different. He played with this question for 10 years. The more he pondered, the more questions arose. Suppose, he asked himself, that you were riding on the end of a light beam and held a mirror before your face. Would you see your reflection?

According to classical physics, you would not— because light leaving your face would have to travel faster than light in order to reach the mirror. But Einstein could not accept this. It didn't feel right. It seemed ludicrous that you would look into a mirror and see nothing. Einstein imagined rules for a universe that would allow you to see your reflection in a mirror while riding a light beam. Only years later did he undertake proving his theory mathematically.

Einstein attributed his scientific prowess to what he called a "vague play" with "signs," "images," and other elements, both "visual" and "muscular." "This comminatory play," he wrote, "seems to be the essential feature in productive thought."

My project of the last 25 years has been to develop techniques and mental exercises, based in part on Einstein's methods, that work in the short term and also develop the mind's permanent powers.

Einstein is the most spectacular modern example of a man who could dream while wide awake. With few exceptions, the great discoveries in science were made through such intuitive "thought experiments."

Inventor Elias Howe labored long and hard to create the first sewing machine. Nothing worked. One night, Howe

had a nightmare. He was running from a band of canni- 130
bals – they were so close, he could see their spear tips.
Despite his terror, Howe noticed each spear point had a
hole bored in its tip like the eye of a sewing needle.

When he awoke, Howe realized what his nightmare
was trying to say: On his sewing machine, he needed to 135
move the eyehole from the middle of the needle down to
the tip. That was his breakthrough, and the sewing
machine was born.

Insights from dreams have inspired rulers, artists, scientists, and inventors since Biblical times. But day after 140
day, year after year, the vast majority of people squelch
their most profound insights without even knowing it.
This defensive reflex—which I call The Squelcher—
blocks us from achieving our full potential.

But dreams have their limitations. They are notorious- 145
ly hard to control. We have not yet learned how to sum-
mon them at will. And, most of the time, we forget them.

In March 1977, a group of us had heard about the rev-
olutionary experiments Russian scientists were making
by tapping the subconscious for accelerated learning. 150
Although no one at that time had published reliable
accounts of the exact procedures, we reconstructed these
as best we could from odd corners of the scientific liter-
ature. We decided to conduct an experiment in a friend's
apartment in Arlington, Va. 155

We were completely surprised. Nearly every technique
produced striking results for almost everyone in the
group. Especially memorable was the experience of a
participant whom I shall call "Mary." Like all of us, she
had agreed to embark upon some new learning experi- 160
ence just prior to the workshop. She chose the violin.
Mary had her first lesson just one week before our exper-

iment. Until that time, she had never touched a violin in her life.

The week following our workshop, Mary had her sec- 165
ond lesson. She worked as a secretary in a Washington office and had only a moderate amount of time to practice. Nevertheless, after Mary had played a few minutes, her astonished instructor announced that he was going to reenroll her in his advanced class! At our second experi- 170
mental workshop, just a few weeks later, Mary gave a fine concert with her violin.

Mary owed her precocious ability to the "Raikov Effect." Using deep hypnosis, Soviet psychiatrist Dr. Vladimir Raikov made people think that they had 175
become some great genius in history. When he "reincarnated" someone as Rembrandt, the person could draw with great facility. Later, the subject remembered nothing. Many would scoff in disbelief when shown artwork they had done under hypnosis. 180

Raikov demonstrated that talents unleashed under hypnosis left significant effects even after the sessions. So the method was more than an experimental oddity. It was a practical tool for learning. Moreover, as we were to discover it could be achieved without the aid of hypnosis. 185

Find the number of lines you read and multiply that by nine. This is your current reading speed.

If you would like to read more, this excerpt was taken from *The Einstein Factor,* (Prima Publishing, Rocklin, California, 1995)

Reading Comprehension Test

The Einstein Factor

(Questions 1-10 apply prior to line 85. Questions 11-20 to the balance.)

1. Einstein suffered from Dyslexia. T F

2. Einstein was expelled from college. T F

3. Einstein published the Theory of Relativity when he was 26. T F

4. Einstein died in 1955. T F

5. Einstein's brain was stored in a jar for 50 years. T F

6. Marian Diamond was a neuroanatomist at the University of California at San Diego. T F

7. Marian Diamond's experiments on rats increased the size of the rats' brains. T F

8. Santiago Ramòn y Cajal is the father of neuroanatomy. T F

9. Einstein believed he had retarded development. T F

10. Einstein was asleep and dreaming when he discovered the Theory of Relativity. T F

11. Einstein practiced trigonometry while hunting with his uncle. T F

12. Einstein used to wonder what it would be like to run beside a beam of light. T F

13. According to classical physics if you were riding at the end of a beam of light with a mirror held in front of your face, you would see your reflection.   T F

14. Einstein attributed his scientific prowess to "vague play".   T F

15. Einstein could dream while he was awake.   T F

16. The inventor, Elias Howe, created the first sewing machine during a dream about cannibals.   T F

17. Russian scientists conducted experiments on the subconscious for accelerated learning.   T F

18. Mary was a secretary in Washington.   T F

19. The Raikov Effect made people think they were dreaming.   T F

20. The Raikov Effect left no effects afterwards.   T F

Answers
1. T, 2. F, 3. T, 4. T, 5. F, 6. F, 7. T, 8. T, 9. T, 10. F
11. F, 12. T, 13. F, 14. T, 15. T, 16. T, 17. T, 18. T, 19. F, 20. F

Since 1981, Learning Forum has produced educational programs for students, educators and business. Its vision is to create a shift in how people learn, so that learning will be joyful, challenging, engaging and meaningful.

Programs and products of Learning Forum—

QUANTUM LEARNING PROGRAMS

Quantum Learning is a comprehensive model of effective learning and teaching. Its programs include: **Quantum Learning for Teachers**, professional development programs for educators providing a proven, research-based approach to the design and delivery of curriculum and the teaching of learning and life skills; **Quantum Learning for Students,** programs that help students master powerful learning and life skills; and **Quantum Learning for Business,** working with companies and organizations to shift training and cultural environments to ones that are both nurturing and effective.

SUPERCAMP

The most innovative and unique program of its kind, SuperCamp incorporates proven, leading edge learning methods that help students succeed through the mastery of academic, social and everyday life skills. Programs are held across the U.S. on prestigious college campuses, as well as internationally, for four age levels: Youth Forum (9-11), Junior Forum (12-13), Senior Forum (14-18), and College Forum (18-24).

SUCCESS PRODUCTS

Learning Forum has brought together a collection of books, video/audio tapes and CD's believed to be the most effective for accelerating growth and learning. The *Quantum Learning Resource Catalog* gives the highlights of best educational methods, along with tips and key points. The Student Success Store focuses on learning and life skills.

For information contact:

LEARNING FORUM
1725 South Coast Highway • Oceanside, CA • 92054-5319 • USA
760.722.0072 • 800.285.3276 • Fax 760.722.3507
email: info@learningforum.com • www.learningforum.com

Bobbi DePorter is president of Learning Forum, producing programs for students, teachers, schools and organizations across the US and internationally. She began her career in real estate development and ventured to co-found a school for entrepreneurs called the Burklyn Business School. She studied with Dr. Georgi Lozanov from Bulgaria, father of accelerated learning, and applied his methods to the school with great results. Having two children and seeing a need to teach students *how to* learn, she then applied the techniques to a program for teenagers called SuperCamp, which has now helped thousands of students relearn how they learn and reshape how they live their lives. In addition to SuperCamp, Learning Forum produces Quantum Learning for Teachers staff development programs for schools, and Quantum Learning for Business for organizations. Bobbi is also a past president of the International Alliance for Learning. She is the author of ten books on the subject of learning. *Quantum Learning: Unleashing the Genius in You, Quantum Teaching: Orchestrating Student Success,* and *Quantum Business: Achieving Success through Quantum Learning* are published in the United States, Great Britain, Germany, Slovenia, Brazil, Russia and Indonesia. These books continue to influence the expansion of Quantum Learning programs and draw international interest.

Mike Hernacki, a former teacher, attorney, and stockbroker, has been a freelance writer and marketing consultant since 1979. He is the author of four books: *The Ultimate Secret to Getting Absolutely Everything You want, The Secret to Conquering Fear, The Forgotten Secret to Phenomenal Success,* and *The Secret to Permanent Prosperity.* His books have been translated into six languages and are sold all over the world. He now divides his time between writing and personal success coaching.